Arctic Tern Migration

by Grace Hansen

Abdo

ANIMAL MIGRATION

Kids

Abdo Kids Jumbo is an Imprint of Abdo Kids
abdobooks.com

abdobooks.com

Published by Abdo Kids, a division of ABDO, P.O. Box 398166, Minneapolis, Minnesota 55439.
Copyright © 2021 by Abdo Consulting Group, Inc. International copyrights reserved in all countries.
No part of this book may be reproduced in any form without written permission from the publisher.
Abdo Kids Jumbo™ is a trademark and logo of Abdo Kids.

Printed in the United States of America, North Mankato, Minnesota.

052020

092020

Photo Credits: iStock, National Geographic Image Collection, Shutterstock

Production Contributors: Teddy Borth, Jennie Forsberg, Grace Hansen
Design Contributors: Dorothy Toth, Pakou Moua

Library of Congress Control Number: 2019956472

Publisher's Cataloging-in-Publication Data

Names: Hansen, Grace, author.

Title: Arctic tern migration / by Grace Hansen

Description: Minneapolis, Minnesota : Abdo Kids, 2021 | Series: Animal migration | Includes online
    resources and index.

Identifiers: ISBN 9781098202286 (lib. bdg.) | ISBN 9781098203269 (ebook) | ISBN 9781098203757
    (Read-to-Me ebook)

Subjects: LCSH: Arctic tern--Juvenile literature. | Birds--Behavior--Juvenile literature. | Flyways--Juvenile
    literature. | Animal migration--Juvenile literature. | Animal migration--Climatic factors--Juvenile
    literature.

Classification: DDC 598.252--dc23

Table of Contents

Arctic Terns

The Arctic tern gets its name from where it is born.

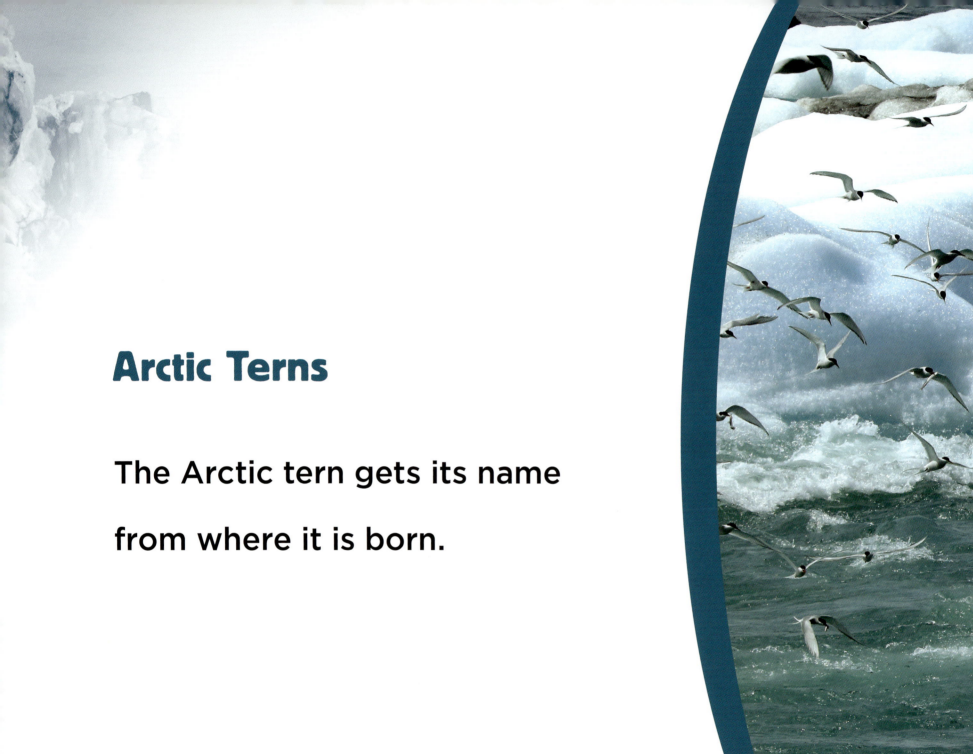

Arctic terns are amazing little birds. They have the longest **migrations** of any animal.

Arctic terns **breed** across the Arctic. They nest in **colonies** and often near coasts.

Arctic terns lay 1 to 3 eggs. After they hatch, parents feed the chicks for about a month. Soon, the chicks will learn to **plunge-dive** for food.

The Longest Migration

Arctic terns spend two to three months in their nesting areas. The young grow stronger in that time. In August and September, they begin a very long journey south to **Antarctica**.

Arctic

Antarctica

13

Arctic terns fly up to 57,000 miles (92,000 km) each year! Like most animals, they **migrate** to find food. They are also avoiding the harsh Arctic winters.

Arctic terns stay in **Antarctica** for up to 5 months. They spend time feeding in the Antarctic waters.

Their **migrations** to and from their winter home include stops. They eat and rest during these stops. This gives them energy for their long flights.

Coming Home

Arctic terns arrive home in May or June. Most of them return to the same place each year.

Arctic Tern Migration Routes

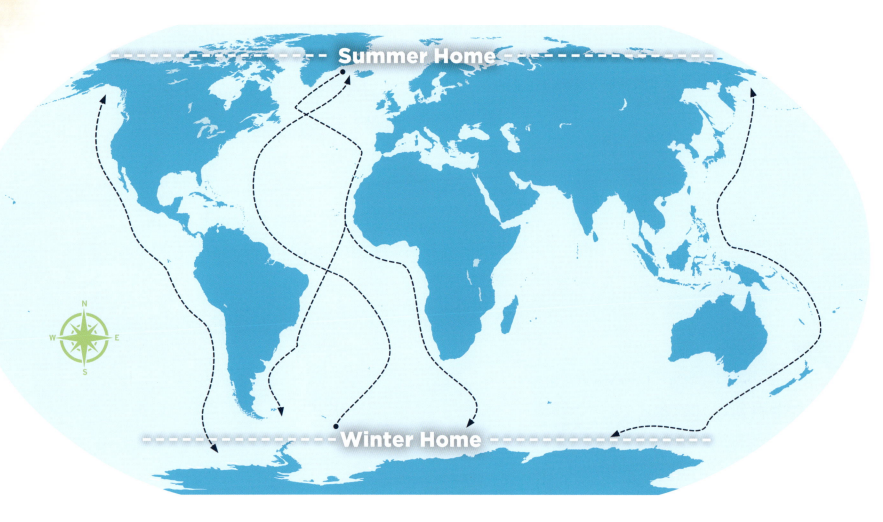

Summer Home

Winter Home

<------> Routes

Glossary

Antarctica – the continent that surrounds the South Pole.

breed – to produce young.

colony – a group of animals of the same type living closely together.

migrate – to move from one place to another for food, weather, or other important reasons.

migration – the act or process of migrating.

plunge-diving – a hunting method used by seabirds to catch fish and other water animals.

Index

Abdo Kids ONLINE
FREE! ONLINE MULTIMEDIA RESOURCES

Visit **abdokids.com**
to access crafts, games,
videos, and more!

Use Abdo Kids code
AAK2286
or scan this QR code!